Puffin Books

START HERE IF YOU WANT TO BE
A BLACK BELT IN KARATE

CONTENTS

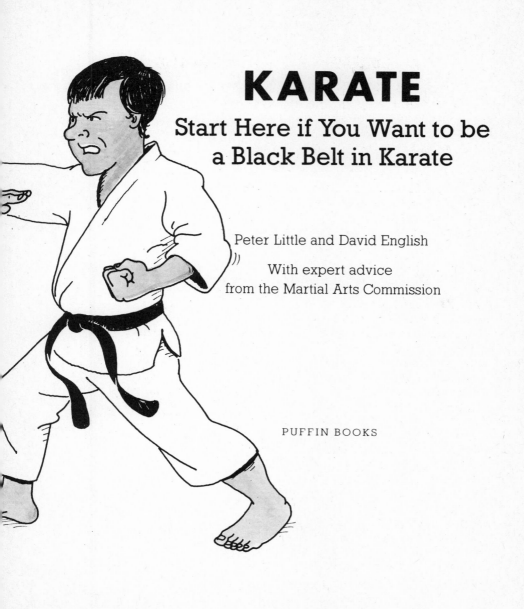

KARATE
Start Here if You Want to be a Black Belt in Karate

Peter Little and David English

With expert advice
from the Martial Arts Commission

PUFFIN BOOKS

1 KARATE – OR, LOOK NO WEAPONS

In Japanese, the word *karate* means 'empty hand'. And that's what karate is – a system of self-defence using no weapons except those that nature has given you – the arm, foot, hand, fist, fingers, knuckles, elbow and head.

When these are used with speed, accuracy and concentration against certain parts of the body, they're just as powerful as any sword or spear. So powerful that the true karateman and woman very rarely use them in real life, and certainly never in anger.

The art of karate came to us from Japan about twenty years ago. But its history goes back much, much further.

2 THE MONKS WITH THE FLYING FEET

Ancient Chinese pictures and books tell us that a possible forerunner of karate came from India to China in the fifth century AD.

An Indian monk named Daruma Taishi is said to have travelled overland from India to China to convert the Chinese to Buddhism. The journey was dangerous and exhausting. At the end of it Daruma was able to teach the Chinese monks a useful system of physical exercise – based on yoga breathing and fist-fighting – that helped them keep physically strong when performing their arduous religious duties. As time went on, the Chinese monks became extremely skilful at fist-fighting, flying and jumping kicks.

Modern karate, though, chiefly owes its birth to a little island just off the Chinese coast, in the seas between China and Japan, and to one islander in particular.

3 A TALE OF THE CHINA SEAS

Okinawa is one of a group of islands that stretch like stepping-stones between China and Japan.

   In the fifteenth century the island was ruled by fierce Japanese overlords. These overlords wouldn't allow the islanders to carry any weapons – especially their native weapon, the *sais*. So they had to invent their own form of self-defence. They used their arms as the shaft of the sword, the hard edges of their hands and feet as blades, and their pointed fingertips as sword-tips.

   This art of self-defence was handed down by word of mouth from generation to generation on the little island.

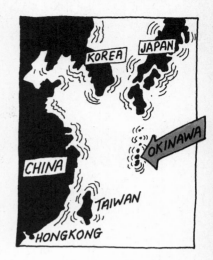

4 THE FATHER OF MODERN KARATE
– FUNAKOSHI GICHIN

In 1880, a boy of eleven, Funakoshi Gichin, learnt the art of
karate from the leading experts on Okinawa. He became an
expert in the art, too, and he it was who wrote down a system of
teaching and learning karate.

Later, in 1917 and 1922, he introduced the art of karate into
Japan. It was in Japan that karate found national and then
worldwide popularity.

5 KARATE – IT'S NOT JUST A MARTIAL ART

Karate is first and foremost a martial art. The blows in karate can disable, even kill, an opponent when used in a dangerous situation. But it's a skill its exponents are reluctant to use in anger. It's such a powerful ability that it gives an exponent a feeling of complete calm, even modesty.

Although it needs speed, strength and agility, it also calls for great mental discipline. That's why many people who take it up also find it a great *total* way of life. They follow it almost like a religion or philosophy. It keeps them bodily and mentally fit. It gives them an excellent means of self-defence. And the movements of karate are often so graceful that, to an outsider, they can make it appear as much an art as a sport.

Karate involves the use of speed, balance and mental concentration to 'focus' a blow (or block and avoid someone else's blow) with tremendous force on a particular target of the body. In practice, these blows (or kicks, if made with the feet) are 'pulled' at the last moment, just short of the target,

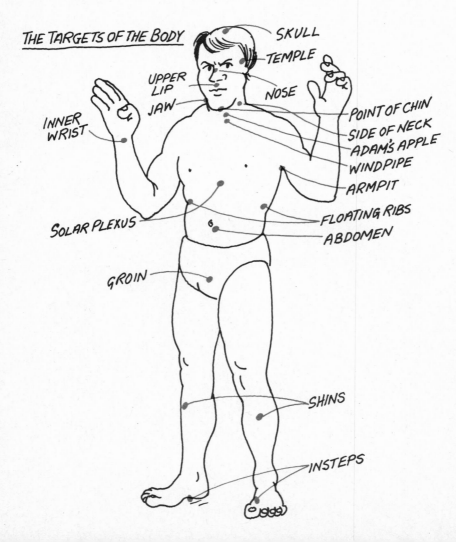

THE TARGETS OF THE BODY

SKULL
TEMPLE
UPPER LIP
JAW
NOSE
INNER WRIST
POINT OF CHIN
SIDE OF NECK
ADAM'S APPLE
WINDPIPE
ARMPIT
SOLAR PLEXUS
FLOATING RIBS
ABDOMEN
GROIN
SHINS
INSTEPS

otherwise they'd be very painful indeed. In reality, they could not just disable, but injure and even kill.

Karate, we repeat, is a skill you'll probably never have to put into use.

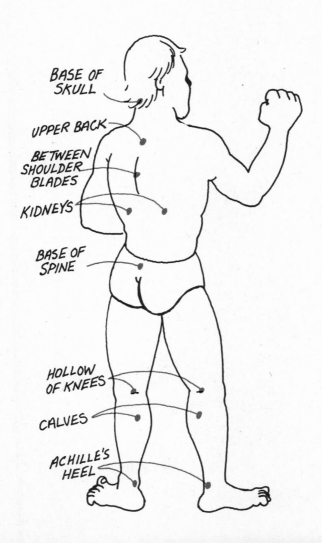

BASE OF SKULL

UPPER BACK

BETWEEN SHOULDER BLADES

KIDNEYS

BASE OF SPINE

HOLLOW OF KNEES

CALVES

ACHILLE'S HEEL

7 A POPULAR MISCONCEPTION SHATTERED AT ONE BLOW

You've probably heard that exponents of karate can break a block of ice, wood or a brick with the side of their hand in one blow. Experts at karate can and do perform such feats. (In fact, some styles of karate like the *kyokushinkai* put great emphasis on these feats.) But they are very much the 'show business' side of karate. And they should on no account be attempted by a beginner.

Anybody, at any age, provided they're pretty fit and have all
their faculties, can learn karate. The younger you start the
better. Six is a good age. Men and women, boys and girls can
do it, although women and girls will probably have less
strength. Karate is an excellent form of self-defence, as well
as a good way of keeping fit.

However, *don't* start to learn karate unless
you're prepared to practise hard, and follow
responsibly the teaching of a good school.

There's only one good place to
learn karate thoroughly. It's not in the
pages of this book, which is only
intended as an introduction to the
sport. It's in a really good *dojo*
or karate training hall.

Before reading any further, you should be warned that karate is a skill never to be used except in really dangerous circumstances, such as tackling a mugger or an armed burglar.

Normally you should never have to use it outside the *dojo*. However, modern life, especially in big cities, is increasingly dangerous, so it's a skill well worth learning.

Karate is a skill that should be learnt from expert instructors in a proper school. Your instructor will not teach you blows that can seriously injure until you reach an advanced stage, when he thinks you're ready and responsible enough to learn them. But even the simpler blows in karate can seriously hurt. Don't practise them on your friends, family or the cat. If you do use them irresponsibly, in anger, and to hurt, you will have learnt nothing about karate.

10 HOW TO CHOOSE A GOOD SCHOOL OF KARATE

You may see small ads in the papers offering karate lessons. Be wary. A lot of these schools are run by people with no qualifications to teach karate. (They sometimes even award themselves a black belt!)

The best way to find a good school is to write to one of the official bodies which control karate in Britain and other countries. (You'll find their addresses in the back of this book.) They'll tell you your nearest school. Go along, judge the atmosphere, ask questions about its teaching and watch for a while before joining.

A good *dojo* will be a clean, disciplined place with a happy atmosphere, run by one or more qualified *sempai* or teachers.

11 KARATE, KUNG-FU, JUDO, KENDO AND JU-JITSU. WHAT'S THE DIFFERENCE?

They're all ancient oriental martial arts. With the exception of kendo (a Japanese art of sword-fighting) they just stress a different aspect of unarmed combat.

Kung-fu is a Chinese martial art that uses both boxing and kicking.

KENDO—AN ANCIENT FORM OF JAPANESE SWORD-FIGHTING WHERE ARMOUR IS WORN

Judo and ju-jitsu are more like wrestling – you can actually perform what you've learned by grappling and gripping and throwing your opponent.

Karate uses all the weapons of the body – hands, fists, feet, elbows, the lot – and teaches you to use them all in coordinated fashion. But there's no wrestling involved, and unlike judo you have to check or 'pull' your blows before they land – for obvious reasons.

A TYPICAL JUDO THROW. THIS KIND OF MOVE YOU'LL NEVER FIND IN KARATE

12 THE DIFFERENT STYLES OF KARATE

You may find your nearest school practises a definite style of karate.

There are many styles.

Some put more emphasis on the mental discipline, the 'philosophy' of karate.

Others put more emphasis on the special stances, on strength, or speed, or competition sparring.

Still others use padded suits and masks in training.

Some allow no competition sparring, considering it dangerous.

Others allow a few selected blows to land.

A few put great pride in their ability to smash bricks, ice or wood.

Whichever kind of school you choose, you should follow its teaching.

13 WHAT YOU WEAR IN KARATE, AND WHY

The traditional outfit you wear in karate is called the *gi*. You can buy it in a sports shop or in the *dojo*. It consists of a white linen or cotton jacket with short sleeves, white trousers and a belt. The jacket and trousers are light and loose-fitting so as not to restrict your movements.

A good karate student will always keep his *gi* clean and well-folded.

The belt tells how advanced a student you are – different belts in different colours distinguish the different grades of *kyu* (student) and *dan* (expert). (But more of the belts later.)

Your feet are bare. Shoes would not only be heavy, but could be dangerous when you perform a kick.

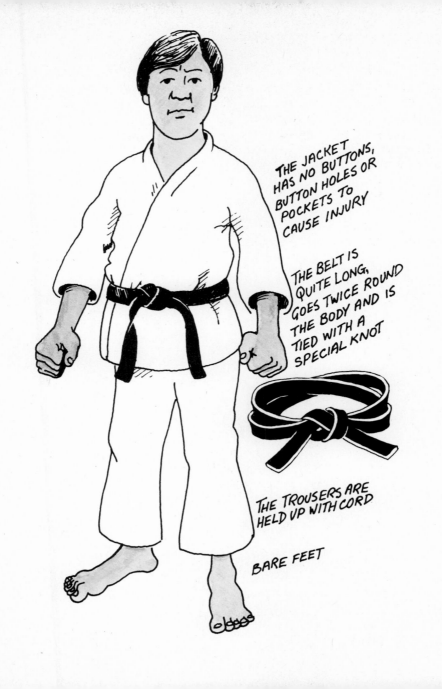

THE JACKET
HAS NO BUTTONS,
BUTTON HOLES OR
POCKETS TO
CAUSE INJURY

THE BELT IS
QUITE LONG,
GOES TWICE ROUND
THE BODY AND IS
TIED WITH A
SPECIAL KNOT

THE TROUSERS ARE
HELD UP WITH CORD

BARE FEET

14 IS KARATE EXPENSIVE?

Not in the least.

Once you've bought your *gi* (about £12), your only other expense will be a small fee the school will charge for lessons. This is usually around £1 an hour. But of course fees vary a little according to the school.

Apart from that, there's no expense. You can practise almost anywhere; on your own or with a friend.

A SEMPAI TAKING A CLASS IN KATA

15 HOW YOU LEARN
– THE TRAINING HALL OR DOJO

You learn karate in a class of other students in the same grade or belt as yourself.

The best training halls have sprung polished wooden floors rather like a good gymnasium. Often, one whole wall will be a mirror, so that students can practise their movements in the reflection. The teacher or *sempai* will take the whole class in a series of exercises or *katas*, and then will give individual advice. You may find the pace of the exercises a bit exhausting at first, if you're not fit, but you'll soon get used to it.

A good karate *dojo* is a well-disciplined place, with a good happy atmosphere. Students treat each other, and the teacher, with courtesy and respect. There's no smoking, or swearing, or eating. This atmosphere of quiet discipline is necessary to instil the right responsibility into the students.

As long as you want to spend on it. You will be graded for belts about every three months. A good student will spend months on each grade or belt, and will practise long and hard. It is possible to reach black belt in about two years, but that's working hard. Fifth dans and upwards are usually awarded to people who've made a real contribution to karate – like discovering a new move or punch.

To the ardent student, karate is a lifelong activity. His or her technique can always be improved upon. There are always new things to learn, always muscles to be toned up, reactions to be quickened, blows to be perfected.

17 THE GRADES OF KARATE

This is an example of the kind of colour-grading that karate exponents are split into.

GRADE	BELT COLOUR
beginner	white
tenth *kyu*	
ninth *kyu*	
eighth and seventh *kyu*	blue
sixth and fifth *kyu*	yellow
fourth and third *kyu*	green
second and first *kyu*	brown
first to fifth *dan*	black
sixth *dan* and upwards	red and white

kyu = student
dan = graduate

Etiquette is very important to karate. It's the courtesy that breeds responsibility and mental character in the student. Most important, it ensures no blow is struck in anger. The karate student bows on entering and leaving the *dojo*. He bows to his opponent before he spars with him. He makes a standing bow to

YOU MUST LOOK AT YOUR OPPONENT

his teacher whenever he meets him inside or outside the *dojo*.

When all the students line up at the beginning and the end of a training session, they do so in grade order, kneel and bow low to the *sempai* or teacher.

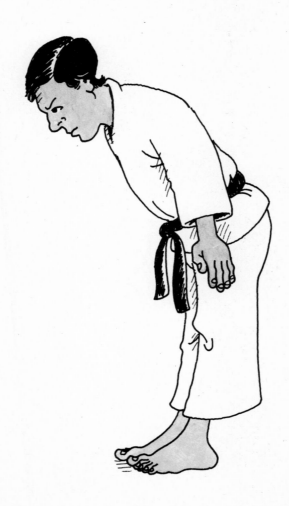

19 THE QUALITIES YOU NEED TO BE GOOD AT KARATE

1 YOU NEED SPEED

The whole aim of karate is to land or block quickly and accurately at a target on your opponent's body before he can counter it. You need speed to avoid your opponent's blows. You also need to recover quickly to attack or block again. Speed of reflex comes with practice.

2 YOU NEED STRENGTH

Accuracy and concentration of force at speed are more important than strength. However, it does pay to have strong hips and legs and your strength will be improved by karate training.

3 YOU NEED CONCENTRATION

Mental and physical concentration combine to concentrate all the muscles of the body into one blow or block. In other words, to concentrate the mind *is* to concentrate the force of the blow.

4 YOU NEED TO BE FIT

Exercises in karate are long and hard. A fat or unfit person has to be eased gently into the full rigours of training. But eventually no sport could be better for you if you're overweight or under-exercised. It'll make you slimmer and fitter, and make your joints supple and flexible.

5 YOU NEED TO PRACTISE HARD

If you can only manage one practice session a week, it would help to practise at home. Many students do some practice every day.

It's easy to get bored by the continuous exercises, but only through them will your karate techniques become 'second nature'. The more you practise, the more automatic they will become.

6 YOU NEED TO BE AGILE

Agility on the feet and excellent balance are essential. These, too, will come from constant training.

7 YOU NEED GOOD BREATH CONTROL

A blow or block in some styles of karate is accompanied by a strong breathing out. This helps you concentrate your total force for that second when you need it, contracting all your muscles.

It is sometimes, too, accompanied by a *kiai* or yell, that acts as a good focus for the blow.

IN GENERAL, ANY HARD BONY PART OF THE BODY CAN BE USED AS A WEAPON

HEAD

FINGERS

HAND

FOREARM

FIST

EDGE OF HAND

WRIST

ELBOW

KNEE

SHIN

SIDE OF FOOT

INSTEP

HEEL

FLAT OF FOOT

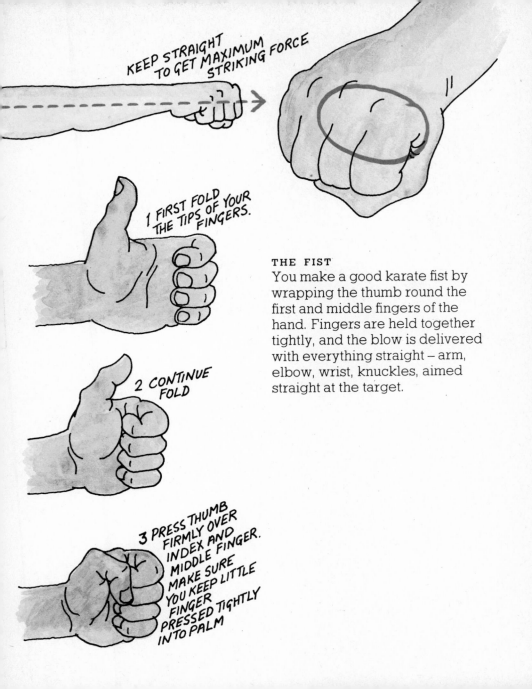

KEEP STRAIGHT TO GET MAXIMUM STRIKING FORCE

1 FIRST FOLD THE TIPS OF YOUR FINGERS.

2 CONTINUE FOLD

3 PRESS THUMB FIRMLY OVER INDEX AND MIDDLE FINGER. MAKE SURE YOU KEEP LITTLE FINGER PRESSED TIGHTLY INTO PALM

THE FIST

You make a good karate fist by wrapping the thumb round the first and middle fingers of the hand. Fingers are held together tightly, and the blow is delivered with everything straight – arm, elbow, wrist, knuckles, aimed straight at the target.

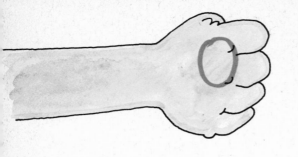

THE BACKFIST
The wrist is slightly bent. You use the two knuckles of the fist adjacent to the thumb to strike with. Good for side attacks, it is characterized by a 'whiplash' movement with a limp wrist.

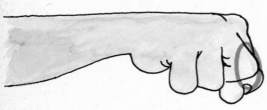

ONE OR TWO KNUCKLE FISTS
Same as normal clenched fist, but you push forward one or two knuckles. The solar plexus or throat are usually the targets.

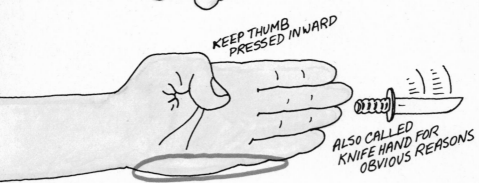

KEEP THUMB PRESSED INWARD

ALSO CALLED KNIFE HAND FOR OBVIOUS REASONS

KNIFEHAND
The 'little finger' side of the hand is used for a 'knife' or a chopping blow.

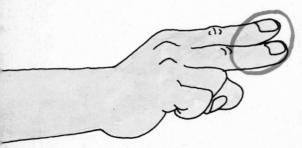

ONE OR TWO FINGER HAND
The outstretched hand, but just using one or two fingers to attack the eyes.

SPEARHEAD
The whole hand outstretched so that the finger tips form a 'spear'. Often aimed at the eyes in self-defence.

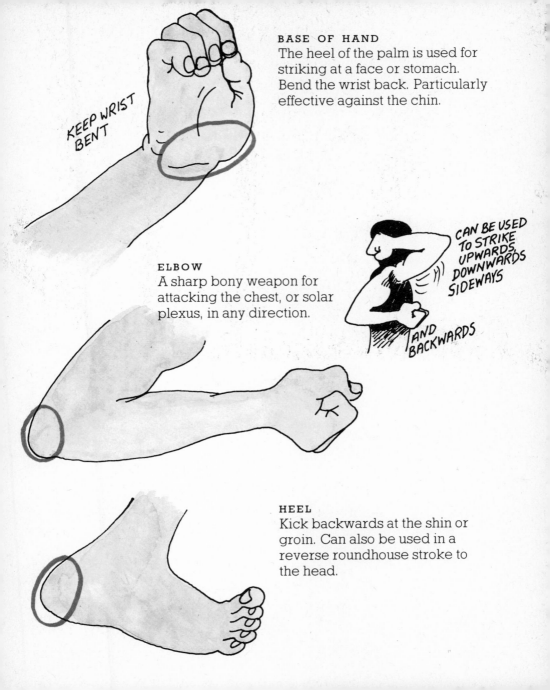

BASE OF HAND
The heel of the palm is used for striking at a face or stomach. Bend the wrist back. Particularly effective against the chin.

KEEP WRIST BENT

ELBOW
A sharp bony weapon for attacking the chest, or solar plexus, in any direction.

CAN BE USED TO STRIKE UPWARDS, DOWNWARDS SIDEWAYS AND BACKWARDS

HEEL
Kick backwards at the shin or groin. Can also be used in a reverse roundhouse stroke to the head.

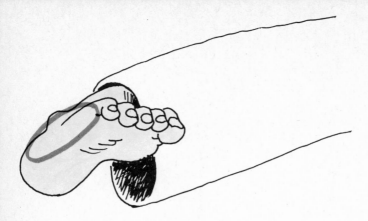

SIDE OF FOOT
Use it like the side of your hand to attack the knee or upper parts of the body.

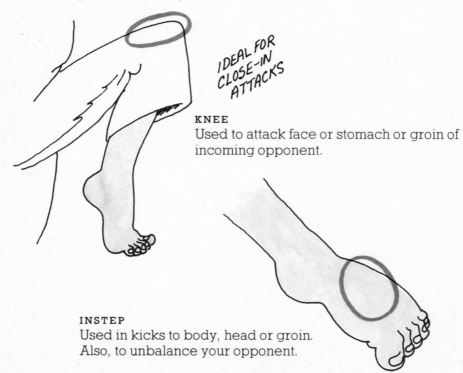

IDEAL FOR CLOSE-IN ATTACKS

KNEE
Used to attack face or stomach or groin of incoming opponent.

INSTEP
Used in kicks to body, head or groin. Also, to unbalance your opponent.

BALL OF FOOT

Used on forward kicks. The toes are turned upwards (or they'll be hurt) in frontward or roundhouse kicks to the neck, ribs or face.

CURL TOES UPWARDS AS MUCH AS POSSIBLE

HAMMER FIST

Use the base of your fist to bring it down on the attacker's head like a hammer. Also very useful as a block.

FOREARM AND WRIST

These obviously make excellent blocking weapons.

HEAD
BUTT YOUR OPPONENT'S FACE OR STOMACH WITH YOUR FOREHEAD OR THE TOP OF YOUR HEAD

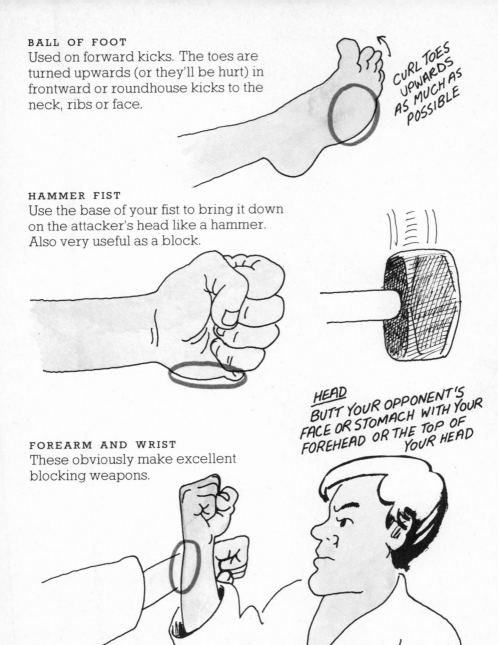

21 SOME EXERCISES TO LIMBER YOU UP

These are to relax and stretch some of the muscles you'll use most often in karate. Start with the legs to limber up your knees. Remember to go slowly at first, to avoid any strain.

LEG STRETCHING
DOING THE SPLITS

LEG STRETCHING
SWING LEGS AS HIGH AS POSSIBLE, STRAIGHT UP

ARM STRETCHING

ROTATE YOUR ARMS IN CIRCLES SIDEWAYS

FIRST ONE WAY THEN THE OTHER

STRETCH AS FAR BACK AS POSSIBLE

BRUSH YOUR EARS WITH YOUR ARMS

ALSO ROTATE YOUR ARMS FORWARDS

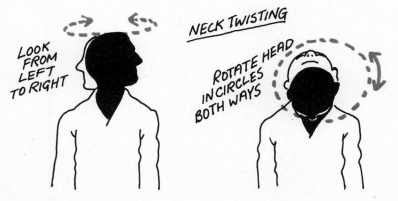

NECK TWISTING

LOOK FROM LEFT TO RIGHT

ROTATE HEAD IN CIRCLES BOTH WAYS

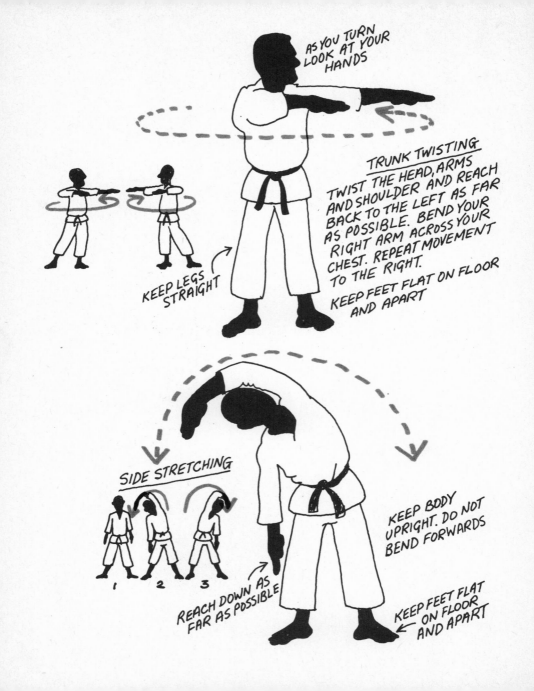

AS YOU TURN LOOK AT YOUR HANDS

TRUNK TWISTING
TWIST THE HEAD, ARMS AND SHOULDER AND REACH BACK TO THE LEFT AS FAR AS POSSIBLE. BEND YOUR RIGHT ARM ACROSS YOUR CHEST. REPEAT MOVEMENT TO THE RIGHT.

KEEP FEET FLAT ON FLOOR AND APART

KEEP LEGS STRAIGHT

SIDE STRETCHING

1 2 3

REACH DOWN AS FAR AS POSSIBLE

KEEP BODY UPRIGHT. DO NOT BEND FORWARDS

KEEP FEET FLAT ON FLOOR AND APART

TRUNK STRETCHING
DO THREE TIMES TO THE LEFT, THEN THREE TIMES TO THE RIGHT, AND SO ON

BEND BODY IN LARGE CIRCULAR MOTION

START WITH HANDS ON HIPS FEET APART

BEND FIRST TO THE LEFT

RIGHT DOWN AS FAR AS POSSIBLE

WHEN UPRIGHT, STRETCH BACK AS MUCH AS POSSIBLE

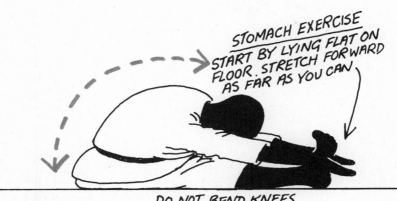

STOMACH EXERCISE
START BY LYING FLAT ON FLOOR. STRETCH FORWARD AS FAR AS YOU CAN

DO NOT BEND KNEES

In karate, you need to be able to move very quickly, yet keep your balance. It's especially important when you kick, for example, to be able to regain your balance, ready for a second attack.

The stances of karate help you keep your balance. Here are just a few of them:

THE FORWARD STANCE

With a straight back and upright head, gaze into the eyes of your opponent.

Keep your feet shoulder-width apart, then take your right foot two shoulder-widths back. Move the rear foot a little sideways.

Face and hips are to the front, and body-weight slightly forwards.

The front knee is flexed, and both knees are tensed outwards.

This is a very good stance from which to block a blow.

STRAIGHT BACK

KNEE SHOULD BE OVER TOES

SHOULDER-WIDTH APART

TWO SHOULDER-WIDTHS APART

THE BACKWARD STANCE

Place your forward foot about 3 ft (90 cm) ahead of the rear foot which takes most of the weight of the body.

The back leg is bent, and the foot placed at an angle of 90 degrees to the front leg.

Legs are tensed outwards a little.

Front knee is raised a little to let the heel lift off the floor.

This is a very good stance from which to kick with the front foot.

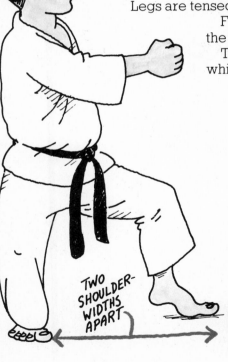

TWO SHOULDER-WIDTHS APART

BACK FOOT 90° TO FRONT FOOT

THE CAT STANCE

Similar to the backward stance, but the front leg is closer to the rear one. Almost all the body-weight is taken on the rear foot.

The front foot is right on its toes and facing forwards.

This is a good stance to use for front kicks, and for quick changes of position.

KEEP BACK STRAIGHT

KEEP MOST OF YOUR WEIGHT ON THE REAR FOOT

BECAUSE MOST OF YOUR WEIGHT IS ON THE BACK FOOT THIS STANCE IS VERY GOOD FOR KICKS

FRONT FOOT POINTS FORWARDS

STRADDLE OR HORSE STANCE

Good for strengthening legs and hips.

Your feet should be one-and-a-half or two shoulder-widths apart.

Knees press outwards over the feet.

(The whole stance is a little like your position when riding a horse.)

Feet are forward-facing and parallel.

Heels are rotated outwards.

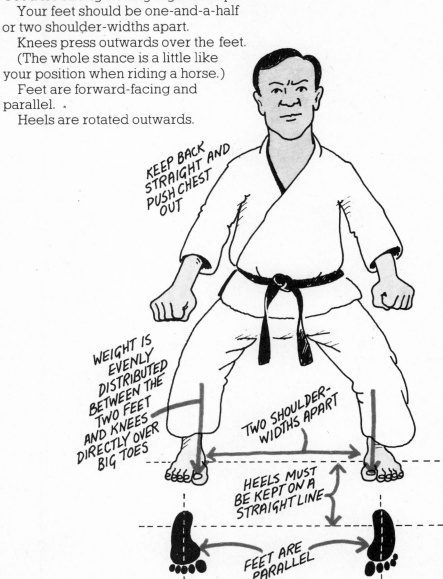

KEEP BACK STRAIGHT AND PUSH CHEST OUT

WEIGHT IS EVENLY DISTRIBUTED BETWEEN THE TWO FEET AND KNEES DIRECTLY OVER BIG TOES

TWO SHOULDER-WIDTHS APART

HEELS MUST BE KEPT ON A STRAIGHT LINE

FEET ARE PARALLEL

The whole aim in karate is to block, punch or kick without losing your balance.

The best way to move is to slide your feet – *not* lift them, except when you kick.

You should also keep hips and head constantly at the same height – there's no bobbing and weaving.

When you turn your body in a different direction, you do so with your *hips*.

Smooth, fluid movement from one stance to another is what a karate expert aims for.

KEEP YOUR BALANCE AT ALL TIMES

KEEP HEAD AT SAME HEIGHT

ALSO KEEP HIPS AT SAME HEIGHT

SLIDE FEET

24 HIPTWIST

This is the smoothest, most supple way of changing your ground in karate.

Jump off the floor, and twist your body from the waist downwards to the left or the right, as you wish to turn.

This increases your ability to turn and change position in mid-air, before attacking your opponent from a different direction. It is rather like a ballet movement and should be performed as smoothly as a ballet dancer would do it.

THE HIPS ARE VERY IMPORTANT IN KARATE. APART FROM GIVING YOU GOOD BALANCE, THEY ADD EXTRA POWER TO YOUR PUNCHING KICKING AND BLOCKING

Punches in karate (with the notable exception of the roundhouse strike) are made absolutely straight.

They are made with enormous speed and, while you punch, your back and hip muscles should be tensed.

REVERSE PUNCH

This is a basic training punch. As you punch with one fist, you retract the other. The reaction force adds strength to the blow. To practise, stand in the forward stance, with your left foot and left fist forward.

When you deliver the punch towards the face or body of your opponent, twist the wrist or forearm to 'focus' the blow, knuckles upwards.

KEEP ELBOW TUCKED IN THROUGHOUT PUNCH

DON'T FORGET THE IMPORTANCE OF THE HIP MOVEMENT (SEE PAGE 45)

KEEP BACK STRAIGHT

KEEP FEET FIRMLY ON GROUND

DO NOT RAISE HEEL

USE ELBOW LIKE A SPRING

KEEP WRIST LOOSE

POINT ELBOW TOWARDS THE TARGET

BACKFIST STRIKE

In this punch the arm is snapped outwards, then snapped back again quickly. Don't extend your arm completely. Make contact with the back of your fist and second knuckles.

ROUNDHOUSE STRIKE

Take up the forward stance with left leg forward and right leg back. The right hand is held back in a fist by your hip. Then you make a strike in an arc at the opponent's left forehead. As you do so, bring the left hand smartly back to give extra power to your punch.

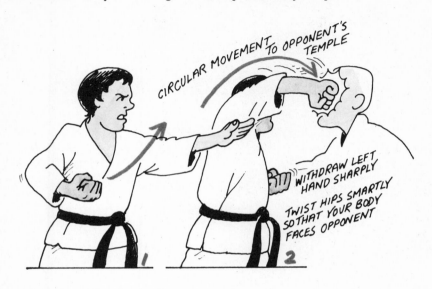

CIRCULAR MOVEMENT TO OPPONENT'S TEMPLE

WITHDRAW LEFT HAND SHARPLY

TWIST HIPS SMARTLY SO THAT YOUR BODY FACES OPPONENT

1

2

STRAIGHT PUNCH

UPPER STRAIGHT PUNCH

MIDDLE STRAIGHT PUNCH

LOWER STRAIGHT PUNCH

WITHDRAW LEFT HAND SHARPLY

TWIST HIPS TOWARDS OPPONENT

1

2

SPEARHAND THRUST
Use the middle three fingers of the hand as a pointed 'spear'. Thrust at the soft parts of the body.

MAKE SURE PALM IS UPWARDS

THE ROTATION OF THE FORE-ARM AND HIPS ARE IMPORTANT

KNIFEHAND STRIKE
Make a 'knifehand' with the 'little finger' side of your hand. Stand in left forward stance, right hand by your right ear, behind the head. The left arm should cover the body. Now swing your striking arm in a swift arc towards your opponent's neck or head, aiming the edge of the hand, and using the snap of your wrist and elbow. As you strike, bring the other hand to your hips palm upwards and wrist bent.

ELBOW STRIKE

You can strike backwards if someone is holding you from behind. You can strike forwards at the jaw or ribs, or aim your elbow at the back when the back is turned.

THIS IS THE BACK ELBOW STRIKE. IT CAN BE USED WHEN YOUR OPPONENT HAS GRABBED YOU FROM BEHIND

WITHDRAW LEFT HAND SHARPLY FOR EXTRA POWER

KEEP ARM CLOSE TO BODY AND ROTATE HIPS

HAND BY EAR ON IMPACT

UPWARD ELBOW STRIKE

Used to strike at the opponent's chin. Step forward on your right leg, then bring right fist up to the side of your neck. For more power, tense the stomach muscles.

Kicks in karate have to be delivered very quickly, and the leg withdrawn again very quickly, or else you will lose your balance. Keep your knee high when you kick.

FRONT KICK
You can either snap your foot from the knee or just thrust it straight at your opponent.

You kick with the ball of your foot at your opponent's abdomen. Keep your toes out of the way or you will hurt them.

The body and supporting left leg should be flexed for better balance and extra range. Take the kicking leg back quickly after impact.

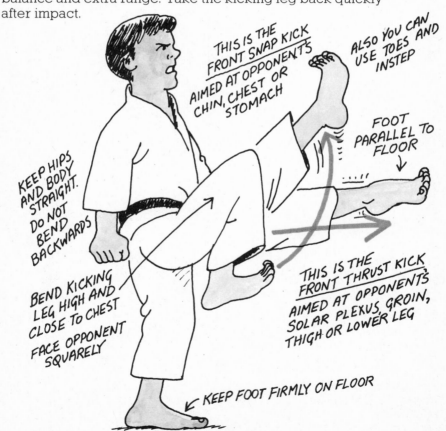

THIS IS THE FRONT SNAP KICK AIMED AT OPPONENTS CHIN, CHEST OR STOMACH

ALSO YOU CAN USE TOES AND INSTEP

FOOT PARALLEL TO FLOOR

KEEP HIPS AND BODY STRAIGHT. DO NOT BEND BACKWARDS

BEND KICKING LEG HIGH AND CLOSE TO CHEST

FACE OPPONENT SQUARELY

THIS IS THE FRONT THRUST KICK AIMED AT OPPONENTS SOLAR PLEXUS, GROIN, THIGH OR LOWER LEG

KEEP FOOT FIRMLY ON FLOOR

SIDE KICK

In this kick, use the edge of your foot. Your support leg needs to be very well balanced. Side kicks involve a lot of swivelling of the hips.

THE SIDE KICK IS USED AGAINST AN OPPONENT COMING FROM THE SIDE. LIKE THE FRONT, YOU CAN EITHER USE A SIDE SNAP KICK OR SIDE THRUST KICK

RAISE KNEE AS HIGH AS POSSIBLE

FOOT FIRMLY ON FLOOR

1 STANCE   2 BEND KNEE   3 KICK!   4 WITHDRAW QUICKLY   5 STANCE. READY FOR NEXT MOVE

ROUNDHOUSE KICK

IMPORTANT TO KEEP HEAD UP

1 2 3 4

Lift your right knee high to one side. Then swing the foot in an arc towards your opponent's head, ribs or neck while swivelling on your left foot. Try and hit your opponent with the ball of your foot. At first, you may only be able to contact with your instep.

Return kicking foot, once again, quickly to its original position, swivelling your hips, but less so than in the side kick.

BACK KICK

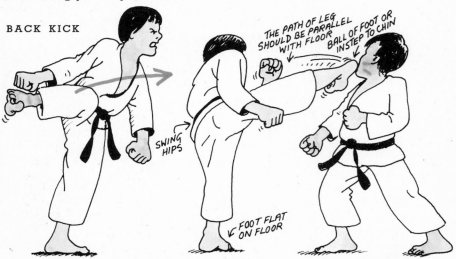

THE PATH OF LEG SHOULD BE PARALLEL WITH FLOOR

BALL OF FOOT OR INSTEP TO CHIN

SWING HIPS

FOOT FLAT ON FLOOR

You need even greater balance for this one. Stand in the normal position. Raise your right knee as though for a front kick, lean your body forward, then kick backwards with your heel towards the stomach or chest.

You'll need to turn your head to look over your right shoulder towards your opponent.

Return kicking foot quickly.

JUMPING KICKS

These are very spectacular but difficult to do. Essentially, you leap into the air at your opponent, kicking either forwards, sideways or back during the high point of your leap. You have to stay balanced in the air (lean into the kick) and come down to the ground again to regain your balance.

THE FLYING SIDE KICK USEFUL FOR ATTACKING THE HEAD OR CHEST. IT IS THOUGHT TO HAVE BEEN FIRST USED TO BRING DOWN A MOUNTED HORSEMAN

To be good at karate, you have to be very good at blocking and avoiding blows and kicks, not just making them. Not only will it stop your opponent's attack, it can put you in a very good position to counter-attack.

A really powerful block can be so painful it can put an opponent out of action immediately – although you cannot win a contest in karate by disabling your opponent.

Some of the great karate experts are simply very good at defending and blocking any attack made on them, thus winning a contest without striking a blow themselves.

Most blocks are made with the hand or arm. Here are some typical blocks.

UPPER RISING BLOCK

Cover your body with your right fist. Put the other fist in front of it. Now quickly raise the left, or blocking arm, as if to ward off a blow to the face, thrusting it hard upwards, using all the power in your body. You will deflect your opponent's blow with the lower part of your forearm.

MIDDLE BLOCK FROM INSIDE

Stand right foot forward, with your right fist by your left armpit. Swing the right arm around, deflecting to the right a blow to your body with the thumb side of the forearm.

MIDDLE BLOCK FROM OUTSIDE

Stand in the forward stance. Your right foot should be forward with the right fist by your right ear. Swing your left elbow quickly across the front of your body to deflect a blow with the small-finger side of your forearm.

LOWER OR DOWNWARD BLOCK

This is used a lot against kicks and punches to the stomach. (You can use all these blocks against kicks, but you'll probably need to use both hands.)

Stand in the forward stance, left hand behind the right ear. Bring the left arm down in a sweep with the outer edge of the forearm near the wrist.

DO NOT SWING ARM BEYOND FRONT OF YOUR BODY

USE HIP TWIST TO DEFLECT KICK

KNIFEHAND BLOCK

Put one hand straight out in front of you. The other (the blocking hand) should be brought up to your ear, palm opposite the ear. Bring the knifehand quickly down and across the chest. At the same time, bring the other hand to your chest, palm upwards. Keep your blocking hand's fingers tight together.

OTHER BLOCKS

A crossed-arm block is a good block to use against kicks and attacks to the face.

You can also block a kick with the open palm of the hand or with your shin.

X BLOCK

WEDGE BLOCK

28 THE BEST WAY TO PRACTISE KARATE – FIND A SPARRING PARTNER

For practising karate, there's nothing better than having a partner to practise your moves against. It helps with timing and it speeds up your reactions.

You can spar in three different ways.

1 BOTH STANDING STATIONARY
Take turns being attacker and defender. Remember always to 'pull' your punches and block at the last second as far as you can.

2 ONE-STEP SPARRING
Both partners should adopt only one stance, for example, the forward-leaning stance, and should then take only one step away from it.

3 THREE-STEP SPARRING
Each partner is allowed only three attacks or blocks.

1 ATTACKER(A) AND DEFENDER(D) TAKE UP STANCE

D →   ← A

2 (A) THROWS A REVERSE PUNCH SEE PAGE 46

3 (D) BLOCKS WITH AN UPPER RISING BLOCK SEE PAGE 54

4 ...AND (D) COUNTERS WITH A LOWER STRAIGHT PUNCH SEE PAGE 47

In competition karate, the contestants fight in a ring eight metres square and are overseen by a referee.

Bouts usually last three minutes with a two-minute extension in the case of a draw.

Open-handed techniques and footsweeps are allowed in competition but only a few karate techniques are permitted. The contestants can aim only at the head and the front and back of the trunk.

If a blow is perfectly aimed, pulled and made and stops just short of contact, the referee will award one point.

If a blow is not 'pulled' and the defender is hit by the blow, the striker can be disqualified.

If no points are scored, the winner can be the contestant who gets the referee's vote.

FOUR JUDGES— ONE AT EACH CORNER

TIME KEEPERS, DOCTORS AND RECORDERS

ONE ARBITRATOR

REFEREE

8 METRES SQUARE

Before there were books on karate, it wasn't easy to hand down the teaching of the art from one generation to another so the *kata* was made up.

A *kata* is a sequence of karate exercises, performed rather like a war-dance, often to simulate an imaginary fight. In fact, when *katas* are performed before the general public, they're as widely applauded as a beautiful dance would be.

The *kata* helps a karate student to remember his stances,

THIS IS TYPICAL OF THE FIRST KATA (YELLOW BELT) YOU SHOULD LEARN. IT HAS THIRTY-SIX MOVEMENTS

AT THE START AND FINISH OF A KATA YOU SHOULD BOW →

1   2

8   9   10   11   12

18   19   20   21   22

28   29   30   31   32

movements, blows and blocks even without a *sempai* present.

There are over fifty *katas* in the different styles of karate. Some are simple ones for beginners, others are for the more advanced student. Some develop breathing, others balance or strength or speed. All simulate an imaginary fight with one or more attackers. The pupil should repeat his *kata* time after time until his movements are smooth, rhythmical and accurate.

Here is a typical one you might well be taught in a beginners' class.

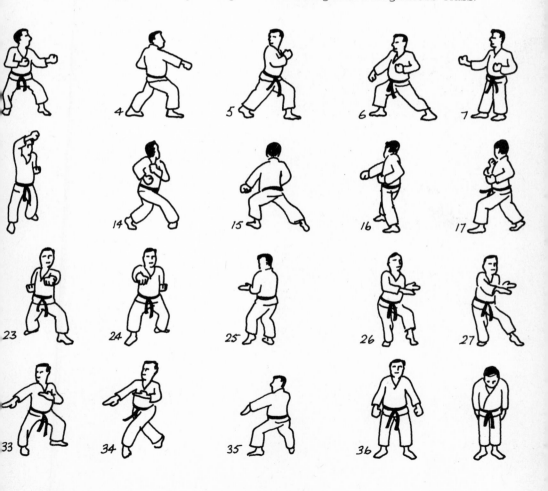

31 HOW TO KEEP FIT OUTSIDE KARATE

A lot of karate students keep fit by following other sports too. Your football, tennis, weight-training, high-jumping, skipping, cycling and running will all be good for your muscles and your reactions.

Karate will, in turn, help you be better and fitter for your other sports.

32 DAILY PRACTICE ON YOUR OWN

Try and practise *katas* on your own at least once a day for half an hour or so. You can practise in your bedroom, in the garden or at school; but don't practise *on* anybody who doesn't know karate.

33 EQUIPMENT TRAINING

Many *dojos* provide training equipment for their students. A punchbag or sandbag is a very good way to practise punches and kicks, especially for timing. A ball swung from a string is also a good target at which to aim kicks.

34 WHERE TO WATCH GREAT KARATE

Did you know that the current world champions in karate are British? You can watch great karate at sports centres like Crystal Palace in South London. The different styles of karate hold their own championships. Look out for announcements of the forthcoming British European and World Championships in the papers and on television.

You can watch good karate being practised at any good training school. Watching someone who's better than you is the best way to learn. If you are going to copy, copy the best.

35 FURTHER READING

Modern Karate by S. Arneil and B. Dowler, Kaye & Ward, 1974
Better Karate by S. Arneil and B. Dowler, Kaye & Ward, 1976
Karate-do by T. Suzuki, Pelham Books, 1975
Karate by Eric Dominy, Teach Yourself Books, English Universities Press, 1967

36 ADDRESSES:
WHERE TO WRITE FOR YOUR NEAREST SCHOOL

The Martial Arts Commission, Broadway House, 15–16 Deptford Broadway, London SE8 4PA
OTHER COUNTRIES
World Union of Karate Organizations, Goram Perssons Vag 19, S-17155 Solna, Sweden

sensei master
sempai teacher
kyu coloured-belt grade student
dan black-belt grade student
dojo training hall
gi suit or outfit
karateka someone learning karate
kata sequence of exercises for attack, defence and counter-attack
kumite contest or sparring bout
shuto edge of hand
shihan headmaster
kiai focus
tori attacker
uke defender

Puffin Books, Penguin Books Ltd, Harmondsworth, Middlesex, England
Penguin Books, 625 Madison Avenue, New York, New York 10022, U.S.A.
Penguin Books Australia Ltd, Ringwood, Victoria, Australia
Penguin Books Canada Ltd, 2801 John Street, Markham, Ontario, Canada L3R 1B4
Penguin Books (N.Z.) Ltd, 182–190 Wairau Road, Auckland 10, New Zealand

Published in Puffin Books 1981
Text copyright © Peter Little, 1981
Illustrations copyright © David English, 1981
All rights reserved

Made and printed in Great Britain by
Hazell, Watson & Viney Ltd, Aylesbury, Bucks
Composition in Rockwell by Filmtype Services Limited, Scarborough, North Yorkshire